W9-ABU-040

Wonders of Nature
Deserts

Dana Meachen Rau

Marshall Cavendish
Benchmark
New York

2

Some people do not like rain. They want to see the sun a lot. They could visit a desert. In a desert, the sun is often in the sky.

Some deserts have lots of sand.
Wind blows the sand and
makes *dunes*.

The Sahara Desert is a sandy desert. It is also the largest desert in the world. It covers one-third of Africa.

Most deserts are rocky.
They might have hills or
mountains. Some have
flat mountains called *mesas*.

Deserts get less than ten inches of rain a year. When it rains, the storm can sometimes come too fast. Water does not have time to soak into the ground. It may dry up quickly in the hot sun.

Most plants and animals need water to live. Even though the desert is dry, it still has many living things.

Plants and animals have
adapted to life in the dry desert.

Desert plants make seeds. These seeds fall and wait for the next rain. After it rains, the seeds start to grow and bloom.

14

Plants have many ways to get water. Some have long roots to get water from deep in the ground. Some plants can hold water in their stems and leaves.

A *cactus* fills up with water when it rains. It gets thinner until it rains again.

Its sharp *spines* stop some animals from stealing its water.

Many desert animals do not
need to drink water. They get
their water from the plants and
animals they eat.

Camels can go a long time without a drink. Kangaroo rats may never drink water their whole life.

An *oasis* may form in the desert. Under an oasis, water is near the surface of the ground. More green plants grow here. People live near an oasis in some deserts.

Deserts are very hot. During the day, animals hide from the hot sun. At night the air is cooler. Animals can come out to eat.

To get out of the sun, squirrels go into *burrows* in the ground.

Lizards and snakes hide under rocks. Larger animals, such as bobcats, find shade in caves.

The desert has some dangerous hunters. Snakes and spiders move across the sand. Hawks fly above looking for rats.

Scorpions kill their *prey* with sharp stingers on their tails.

You might think a sunny day is fun. But in the desert, animals need to fight to stay alive. You might rather live where it is easy to get a glass of water!

Challenge Words

adapted (uh-DAPT-ed)—Changed to make living easier.

burrows (BUR-ohs)—Underground holes dug by animals.

cactus (KAK-tuss)—A spiky desert plant that holds water.

dunes (DOONS)—Hills of sand formed by wind.

mesas (MAY-suhs)—Flat-topped mountains.

oasis (oh-AY-sis)—A place in the desert where there is a lot of water and plant life.

prey (PRAY)—An animal or insect other animals kill for food.

scorpions (SKOR-pee-uhns)—Animals with eight legs and a long tail with a stinger at the end.

spines (SPINES)—The thin, sharp points sticking out of a cactus.

Index

Page numbers in **boldface** are illustrations.

With thanks to Nanci Vargus, Ed.D., and Beth Walker Gambro, reading consultants

Marshall Cavendish Benchmark
99 White Plains Road
Tarrytown, New York 10591-9001
www.marshallcavendish.us

Text copyright © 2008 by Marshall Cavendish Corporation

Library of Congress Cataloging-in-Publication Data

Rau, Dana Meachen, 1971–
Deserts / by Dana Meachen Rau.
p. cm. — (Bookworms. Wonders of nature)
Summary: "Provides a basic introduction to deserts,
including geographical information and plant and animal life"—Provided by publisher.
Includes index.
ISBN-13: 978-0-7614-2667-7
1. Desert ecology—Juvenile literature. 2. Deserts—Juvenile literature. I. Title. II. Series.
QH541.5.D4R38 2007
577.54—dc22
2006038623

Editor: Christina Gardeski
Publisher: Michelle Bisson
Designer: Virginia Pope
Art Director: Anahid Hamparian

Photo Research by Anne Burns Images

Cover Photo by *Corbis*/Kazuyoshi Nomachi

The photographs in this book are used with permission and through the courtesy of:
Peter Arnold: pp. 1, 13 Kevin Schafer; p. 2 Erez Herrnstadt; p. 5 BIOS/Ruoso Cyril; p. 10 Ullstein-Caro;
p. 14 BIOS/Delfino Dominque; p. 17 Fritz Polking; p. 18 Jacken Tack. *Corbis*: p. 4 Sergio Pitamitz;
p. 7 George H.H. Huey; p. 8 John Garrett; pp. 11, 27 Frans Lemmens/zefa; p. 16 Layne Kennedy;
p. 19 Joe McDonald; p. 21 Gallo Images/Sharna Balfour; p. 22 Peter Johnson; p. 25 Jonathan Blair;
p. 26 Michael & Patricia Fogden; p. 29 Sandra Seckinger/zefa. *Photo Researchers*: p. 24 Gerald C. Kelley.

Printed in Malaysia
1 3 5 6 4 2